In His Hands

In His Hands

Insights from Women

DESERET
BOOK

SALT LAKE CITY, UTAH

Library of Congress Cataloging-in-Publication Data
In his hands.
     pages cm
   Writings by Mormon women on various aspects of their relationship with Christ.
   ISBN 978-1-62972-123-1 (hardbound : alk. paper)
   1. Jesus Christ—Meditations. 2. Christian life—Mormon authors. 3. The Church of Jesus Christ of Latter-day Saints—Doctrines. 4. Mormon Church—Doctrines.
   BX8643.J4I5 2015
   248.4'89332—dc23   2015

Printed in China
RR Donnelley, Shenzhen, China

10   9   8   7   6   5   4

Contents

trust 1

discipleship 29

service 53

peace 77

prayer 101

love 127

trust

G.I. Jane

By
Jane Clayson Johnson

When I was anchoring The Early Show on CBS, our producers decided we should replicate the adventures of some of our guests who had been participants on a reality show. In one episode, the guest had faced the challenge of being put through an obstacle course that was set up by an army special forces officer. Well, the producers thought it would be great if I went through an obstacle course too, a mini boot camp of sorts.

To warm me to the idea, they affectionately started referring to me as G.I. Jane and sent me off to West Point for a little boot camp of my own. So there I was, a fairly out-of-shape, not terribly athletic woman, at this very prestigious military academy where real soldiers go to train for battle. I showed up, and I was immediately outfitted in army fatigues and boots and assigned a real, honest-to-goodness drill sergeant.

With cameras rolling, the first thing that Sergeant Wright said to me was this: "Jane, we're going to ask you to do things here that you otherwise thought you couldn't do. That's what this is all about. And I will be here to help you."

So Sergeant Wright started me out easy, or so he thought. Pull-ups were first (I could barely finish one); push-ups were next (I could do about three); and then we had sit-ups, and on and on, and then the obstacle course came. Climbing up a rope ladder. Stepping across wet, moss-covered logs. Crawling on my belly in the mud under a blanket of barbed wire about a foot off the ground. And as I wended my way through this course, I realized it was getting harder and harder and more exhausting and really very challenging. But every time I would get frustrated or tired or scared or just plain stuck, Sergeant Wright was right there. He talked me through it. He was anxious to help me and to encourage me and to give me instruction, and, as he reminded me many times, he had helped many a scared soul through this daunting adventure.

The last section of this obstacle course was

referred to as "walking the plank." Picture a board about twenty feet long, about ten inches across, about three stories *up*. Three stories up! I had to walk the plank—that was my last test. That plank was my bridge to the other side, and it didn't seem to matter much to me that there was a net underneath. I wasn't really thinking about that so much as I climbed up that huge ladder to the top. There I was, with my feet positioned to walk the plank, and the thought of completing this task was completely overwhelming to me. *I cannot do this,* I thought. *I don't WANT to do this,* I thought. *Why do I HAVE to do this?* My head was spinning. I was absolutely stuck. I could not move; I literally was frozen. All I wanted to do was run.

As I stood there, completely frozen in my fear and confusion, I heard one voice that seemed to ring out. It was Sergeant Wright. His strong, calm, comforting voice penetrated my mind, and this is what he said, "Jane! Stop and listen. I am here." *Stop and listen. I am here.* I couldn't see his face, but I could hear his voice loud and clear. And I trusted him. Slowly, methodically, kindly, he talked me across that plank until I was safely to the other side.

I think of that story often as a metaphor for our lives. I think of a loving Heavenly Father saying,

"I'm going to ask you to do things that you otherwise thought you couldn't do. That's what this is all about. But I will be here to help you."

It is a complicated and exhausting and scary world out there, with a lot of loud, penetrating voices competing for our attention. It's so easy to get distracted and to get diverted from the One Voice that is really most important for us to follow. I need to remind myself often to *stop and listen.* •

We cannot ever stop petitioning the Lord for the *righteous desires of our heart.* When we stop petitioning, we run the risk of no longer wanting. And the tragedy of life isn't not getting what you want—it's not wanting it anymore.

—LAUREL C. DAY

Of course we all pray for protection and safety. But for some of us, a preoccupation with staying safe keeps us from realizing just how *resilient* we are. Growing up is in part about learning that we can stand hurt and disappointment, and that they don't mean that we're stupid or undeserving or not being properly taken care of by God. In fact, it was Satan who promised us that he could keep us free from challenges and fear. In contrast, God tells us that the *journey* to our promised land will be fraught with *ferocious storms* and *terrible winds*. He doesn't tell us this to frighten us. He tells us this so that we can know He knows the end from the beginning and we can afford to *trust Him* with our lives here.

—WENDY ULRICH

Unfulfilled Expectations

By
Camille Fronk Olson

"or he maketh sore, and bindeth up: he woundeth, and his hands make whole" (Job 5:18).

I find that pattern very often in scripture, of times when the Lord somehow breaks something down and then builds it back up. I think one of the symbolic ways that is shown is in the idea of barrenness in the scriptures. You can't read the Old Testament very far without noticing that just about every woman you encounter has a challenge with being barren: Sarah, Rebekah, Rachel. I find myself saying, What is this? Even in the very beginning of the New Testament saga, you see Elisabeth, who is barren. And then, often when it is least expected, this incredible blessing of bearing a child is given.

I'd like to say barrenness is symbolic of all those unfulfilled expectations, promises of the Lord, times when He puts us in those difficult circumstances that allow us to put greater trust and faith in Him. Maybe that challenge is having no children. Maybe it's no marriage—or no marriage for a long, long, long time. Maybe it's not having good health. Maybe it's not having opportunities to learn. I remember reading in President Gordon B. Hinckley's biography where, as a young man, dreaming of advanced education and never having an opportunity to get advanced degrees, he said, "I seriously wondered what was going to happen to my life, simply working for the Church."

We have a pretty myopic idea about what may be happening in our lives. God has the full picture, and He seems to put us through the test to see, Will we stay true to Him? And the joy is all the greater when He gives that test and we endure it successfully.

All of us experience a variety of circumstances, but the important thing is that we begin to see the Atonement of Jesus Christ as the *power* that gives us *strength to carry on.*

—CAROLYN J. RASMUS

By the world's standards, we live a linear progression, which means this happens, and then this happens, and then this and this and this, and then we die. There is this *straight line* of lifetime experience. But you know there isn't anyone on earth who really has a linear existence. Every time the Lord reaches to lift us up, the heavens open and our lives go back into the *eternal realm* of which we are so much a part even today. That's what it means to have Christ lift us up: to recognize that there is *higher power* and *higher purpose* in what we're doing here.

—HEIDI SWINTON

A Sure Foundation

By
Ardeth Kapp

Some time ago I was in Phoenix, Arizona, at my niece's home, helping with her three little boys while a new one arrived on this planet earth. Trying to keep them happily occupied while their mom was in the hospital, I was sitting with them at the kitchen table one day painting rocks. We were painting bugs and bees and butterflies and whatever else came to mind when we heard footsteps approaching the front door. The boys knew it was their mom and dad with their baby brother. They rushed to the door, and their parents came in, and the boys took turns holding this little brother in their arms. It looked to me as if they almost knew each other. Maybe they remembered somehow.

After the boys had each taken a turn holding the baby, they came back to the table. We started painting rocks again, and then little Josh, five years old, looked at me and said, "Nana Ardie, how many birthdays do you have left?"

I said, "Josh, I don't know. Why do you ask?"

And he said, "Because I love you, and I don't want you to ever die."

I said, "Oh, Josh, let me tell you something wonderful. You see, because Jesus came to earth and did all that He was asked to do, was obedient to the plan, He made it possible so that when I go back to Utah, I'll keep loving you, and we'll look forward to when we can get together again."

And he said, "Oh, okay." And then he just went back to painting with his paintbrush.

It is the truth: Jesus did make it possible for us. Families are to be together forever. We just have to stay on the path. If Josh had been a little older, I would have proceeded just a little further with the testing, and I would have looked at those little boys, and I would have said what Helaman said to his sons, "Remember, remember that it is upon the rock of our Redeemer, who is Christ, the Son of God, that ye must build your foundation; that when the devil shall send forth his mighty winds, yea, his shafts in the whirlwind, yea, when all his hail and his mighty storm shall beat upon you, it shall have no power over you to drag you down to the gulf of misery and endless wo, because of the rock upon which ye are built, which is a sure foundation, a foundation whereon if men build they cannot fall" (Helaman 5:12).

What a promise! What a foundation! What a rock! Of course we are going to have storms in our lives. This is no ordinary time. The world is in chaos, and we are called to make a difference. We really are. This isn't an easy time, but the Lord is counting on us. And we can count on Him to be a sure foundation for us. ●

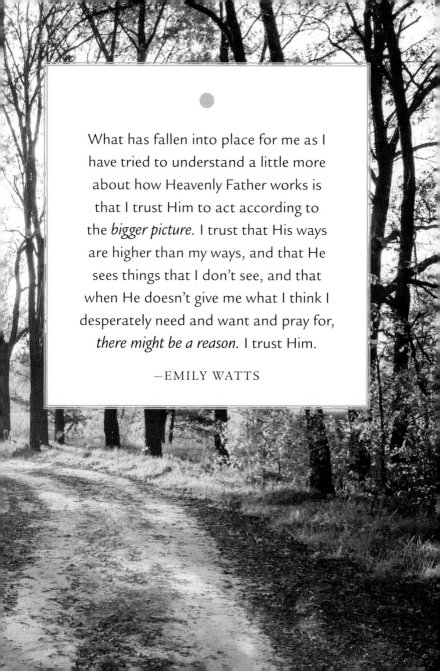

What has fallen into place for me as I have tried to understand a little more about how Heavenly Father works is that I trust Him to act according to the *bigger picture*. I trust that His ways are higher than my ways, and that He sees things that I don't see, and that when He doesn't give me what I think I desperately need and want and pray for, *there might be a reason.* I trust Him.

—EMILY WATTS

The Lord Had Better Plans

By

Whitney Permann

I had my life all planned out. As a senior in high school, I planned to follow a dream and be a cheerleader at Ricks College. End of story. But when our elite choir got invited to sing in New York City's Carnegie Hall the *exact* same day as the college tryouts, I was faced with a very painful dilemma.

I had to choose.

I had to choose between two good things. Two dreams. Two loves. It seemed horribly unfair. I couldn't imagine surrendering a lifelong dream to cheer in college, but neither could I fathom turning down an opportunity to sing in Carnegie Hall. Either decision left my young heart grief-stricken; either way I lost something dear. There was nowhere to go but my knees.

I prayed, fasted, counseled with my parents, and

got father's blessings. It was the first time I had really sought the Lord's will for my life—because, for the first time, things weren't going according to plan.

After a great spiritual wrestle, I decided to go to New York—and thus with a heavy heart close the door on the "cheerleading chapter" of my life. I held onto the hope that this was the right decision. Even so, as the choir bus pulled out of the parking lot on its way to NYC a few weeks later, I leaned my head against the window and sobbed. Everything inside of me screamed to get off that bus.

But I didn't. I sang Handel's *Messiah* in historic Carnegie Hall on Palm Sunday. I humbly (if stubbornly) surrendered my will to the Lord, then asked, "What now?" Little did I know how big His plans were for me.

Since I wouldn't be cheering as planned, I decided instead to audition for a show choir at Ricks College called "Showtime Company." Miraculously, I made the choir, and I enjoyed some of the choicest experiences of my life as a member of this group. My testimony of the Savior exploded. I learned how to reach out to others and share the gospel through music. One year in Showtime gave me more than a dozen years of college cheerleading ever could have.

But the biggest blessing of this group wasn't the performing or the touring or even the friends. It was Rock Permann—another member of the choir. Rock, who came from a family of BYU fanatics, was devastated to be the only sibling not accepted to the Y. Faced with his own change in plans, he attended Ricks College instead, became a member of Showtime Company, and met me.

Two years later, we were married.

Looking back on my path, I am certain that the Lord guided me directly to him. All the tears, the pain, the heartache, the questions, the unknowns . . . they were all leading me to him. Yes, I had good—*great*—plans for my life, but the Lord had bigger, better, and more beautiful plans in mind.

It's quite a startling thing to realize that something is not going to happen as you thought it would. It is shocking to know that you have to change, that things will be different. (How does that saying go? "When you make plans, the Lord laughs"?) It might be a job that wasn't offered, a relationship that didn't work out, or a home that was lost. It could be an unanswered prayer, a missed opportunity, or a dream that never came true.

We must trust that someday—if not in this life,

for sure in the next—we can look back and see how all the twists and turns in the road make sense—how they all worked together to lead us to where we were supposed to be all along. We must trust that God knows what He's doing. And maybe—just maybe—we should loosen the grip we have on our own plans and dreams, and have faith that He can exchange "beauty for ashes" (Isaiah 61:3).

After all—He's got it all planned out. •

It takes a lot of *faith*
to put everything you
have on the altar of God,
trust in Him, and know that
His plan is better for you
than the plan you have
mapped out for yourself.

—JANE CLAYSON JOHNSON

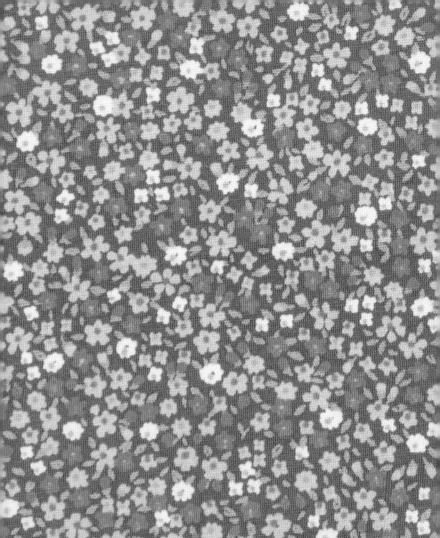

discipleship

What Are You
NOT Doing?

By
Carolyn J. Rasmus

I am an adult convert to the Church. On a trip to Detroit after my baptism, I went to lunch with a really good friend, a friend I'd known for years, and we talked a lot about my conversion. One of the things that she said in parting was, "Carolyn, you know, quite frankly, I don't care what church you belong to. But I don't think *you* believe you made the right decision." You know, somebody has to plant only about that much doubt in your head and in your heart, and pretty soon you're saying, "Did I?"

Then I saw someone else, who said to me, "Well, I hear they brainwashed you out there." And someone else said, "I can't believe you would join that church—the Mormons, of all people, the cult people." Well, I tell you, when I got on the plane to go home, I was absolutely shattered, and I began to wonder if I'd been brainwashed and if I had made a mistake.

I walked around in an absolute stupor for at least three weeks. I don't even know what happened. It got to the point where I could hardly get dressed, I was so confused and uptight. I finally went one day to the man who had baptized me, and I said, "Brother K., joining your church is the worst decision I've ever made."

Well, he straightened me out right away. "This is not my church," he said. "This is The Church of Jesus Christ of Latter-day Saints, restored as it was in the New Testament in these latter days." And then he looked at me, and he asked me a question: "Carolyn, what are you *not* doing that prevents the Spirit of the Lord from being with you?"

I just looked at him. I thought, *I'm not doing anything wrong.* And then he said to me, "Are you praying, sincerely praying? Are you reading the scriptures?"

Well, of course I said no. He admonished me to go home and begin right then. "Read one chapter," he said, "in the Book of Mormon tonight before you go to bed. Pour out your heart to your Heavenly Father and tell Him how you feel. And then stay on your knees and listen for an answer."

I know you're waiting for me to tell some miraculous thing that happened: the light appeared, the room that was dark grew light, or something. Well, to be honest with you, nothing like that happened. But gradually, day by day by day, as I kept this up, I came to the point where one day I thought, "You know what? I'm beginning to feel normal again." And then one day I was walking across campus and I thought, "I think I'm going to be okay." I began to feel at peace. Through those little, tiny baby steps of doing just a little bit every day, my faith began to grow. ●

I think our job is to do our best in whatever circumstance God places us in, to be happy, to be positive, to help others, to be cheerful, and not to cry ourselves to sleep more than once a month— okay, twice (except in February because it is shorter).

—MARY ELLEN EDMUNDS

God's Will,
Our Choice

By
Laurel C. Day

I 've spent a lot of my life a little obsessed with the notion of figuring out "God's will"—as if there were some master, mapped-out plan out there and my entire life job was to figure it out and just be willing to do it.

I believed God had such a specific plan for my life that every time a choice came up, I didn't really ever consider what I wanted. Because my job was to follow His will . . . what HE wanted.

But during a critical time in my life, the thought occurred to me that perhaps that way of looking at my life was a cop-out—a way to abdicate the real obligation of my life: to CHOOSE.

Sometimes it feels like a tricky line, doesn't it? We are here to "act and not be acted upon" (2 Nephi 2:26). And yet, I wanted God to "act upon" me. We are invited to do "many things of [our] own free will" (D&C 58:27). And yet, we don't often trust our ability to choose. At least for me, I spent most of my life only knowing I could trust God and His plan for my life.

I've learned that God does have a plan for my life. And it's a big plan . . . with a capital "P." But I've come to see that there is a little plan, with a lowercase "p," that is entirely mine to live.

At one of the most critical crossroads in my life, while asking to know the Lord's will, I felt like I heard the question: "What do YOU want?"

It startled me.

"Really? I get to choose?" my heart questioned.

I stated as clearly as I could what I wanted and said, "If this really can fit into Thy Plan for me, this is what I choose."

And then I watched something I never would have believed unfold. And I learned God trusted me.

HE. TRUSTED. ME. He trusted me to choose my life.

I am not saying that everything that exists in our lives is our choice. There are some things—some hard things, some disappointing things—that are a result of life circumstances or others' choices. When that is the case, God can and will use those things to help us learn and progress and grow.

But I have come to understand that God's will is not some mysterious list of things He wants us to figure out. Rather, I deeply believe that God's will—what He really wants for us—is to learn how to exercise our own. ●

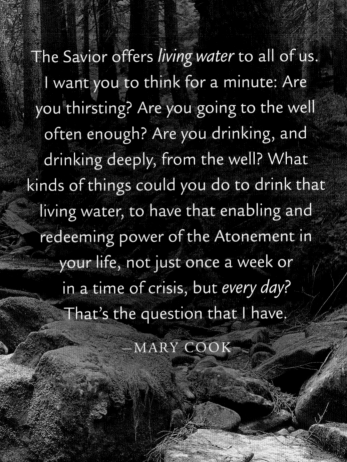

The Savior offers *living water* to all of us. I want you to think for a minute: Are you thirsting? Are you going to the well often enough? Are you drinking, and drinking deeply, from the well? What kinds of things could you do to drink that living water, to have that enabling and redeeming power of the Atonement in your life, not just once a week or in a time of crisis, but *every day*? That's the question that I have.

—MARY COOK

The "Vital Signs" of Conversion

By
Mary Ellen Edmunds

Have you ever been in a gathering where the teacher asked for all those who were converts to raise their hands? Did you have the urge to join the group? I've wondered, if I don't raise my hand, what am I? A not-yet-converted?

Maybe someday I'll be in a gathering and ask, "Will all those who are desirous of experiencing conversion please stand?"

Conversion is a process. I'm "in process." Maybe you are too.

President Harold B. Lee gave a description of what a person is like when he or she is truly converted: "One is converted when he sees with his eyes what he ought to see; when he hears with his ears what he ought to hear; and when he understands with his heart what he ought to understand. And what he ought to see, hear, and understand is truth—eternal truth—and then practice it. That is conversion" (*Stand Ye in Holy Places* [1974], 92).

One thing that strikes me about this is that we're to see, hear, and understand truth—*and then practice it*. "Practice makes perfect," and on the way to perfect it can make us better.

Conversion is about change. It's about thinking, speaking, and acting differently as a result of what we're learning and feeling through our prayers and study, our faith in Jesus Christ. It's about considering more often what the Savior would do and what He wants us to do, and then acting. Practicing. Trying a little harder.

Conversion is being born again—becoming Christlike and Godlike. It's the experience of a mighty change of heart.

As a nurse I used to record "TPR" on patients. These were their vital signs: temperature, pulse, and respiration. If any of these was absent, either my watch was broken or the patient had "left the room." The signs really *were* VITAL.

It's much easier to measure how many times a heart beats per minute than to measure how my heart might be changing in the conversion process.

How do I record how deeply my heart feels about the Atonement of Jesus Christ, about having Him as my Savior and Redeemer? Am I making an honest effort to understand all of this better and to have it change me?

Maybe I can watch myself. Take notes of the vital signs. Do I observe any changes in my thoughts? Am I planting good words in my heart?

I'd like to suggest a couple of questions that have helped me to zero in on a whole list of things I can work on. (I'm not bored!) These are questions I can ask in my communication with my Heavenly Father: "Is there anything I'm doing that's not right for me?" "Is there anything I'm not doing that I need to be doing?" I get a lot of help in setting goals! (Sometimes I whisper things like, "Could You just mention one or two at a time?")

I can think of lots of things I want to work on, but I'm trying to narrow them down to a couple of things that I feel will be possible in the short term. Want to join me? Let's each choose one thing we can work on. Let's become converts! May our "vital signs" reflect that we are in the process of becoming who we are meant to be. •

When you embark on a journey of discipleship, you need to be prepared to leave something behind. Several of the original twelve disciples "left their nets" or "left their ship" or "left all." A similar pattern is found with women, too: the woman at the well in John 4, the story of Ruth, the story of Esther, and even our first mother Eve—stories of people who gave up what they had and left their "comfortable" lives to be disciples of the Lord Jesus Christ.

So what for us? What does discipleship require of us? Leaving our nets? Leaving our ships? Leaving behind all that we have? Perhaps in today's world, being true disciples simply (and not so simply) requires us to leave a bit of ourselves so we can become who we are really meant to be—which is really what discipleship is all about.

In order to become who you really are, you need to be willing to let go of who you are not.

—LAUREL C. DAY

Showing Up

By
Virginia H. Pearce

One of the good choices we can make in this life is just to show up. You may think that "showing up" means you have to do something, you have to be useful. When my mother aged, just like almost every elderly person you've ever known, one day she complained, "This is so discouraging. I'm just not useful to anybody. I'm not doing a darn thing for anybody." And I said, "Oh, Mother, are you kidding me? Every time you walk into a room, it gets better for all of us. Your very presence makes a difference to us."

That's what "showing up" is: it's showing up with your spirit for other people. You and I are still alive. We're not dead yet—which means that we still have a mission to perform. We are still useful. I don't know whether it's babysitting or just walking into a room and elevating the spirit in that room, but I truly be-lieve that as long as we're on this earth, it means the Lord says we haven't finished what we need to do. So we never need to feel that we're not useful, and we always need to know that we can make a choice to show up. We can show up and serve God. •

If we wait for the pressures
of the latest sale, or the
latest movie, or the latest
whatever to decide what we
are going to do, we are out of
control, and that violates our
human nature. We need to
be *accountable* for ourselves.
If we don't take charge,
everything else will take charge.

—ARDETH KAPP

service

"I Can Help You"

By
Heidi Swinton

Sometimes we can do something huge and magnanimous; sometimes what we do is fairly simple and straightforward but can make all the difference.

I walked into Relief Society one morning a number of years ago, when I was working on a project about the Prophet Joseph Smith. I was writing a documentary for PBS and a book about it. I was working so hard on this that I didn't do much else. I had teenage sons at home, and I was in a flurry all the time, meeting needs and carpooling and feeding people, doing this and doing that—and writing. I stayed up all night Tuesday nights because I needed that extra time, and that was the only place I could find it.

So, on the morning in question I raced into Relief Society and sat down in my chair. I didn't know if my hair was even combed; I probably didn't have on shoes that matched. It was kind of like that. I turned, and who was I sitting next to but Eileen. Eileen, who had white rugs in her house. What does that tell you?

Eileen looked at me and asked, "How are you today?" That's kind of a standard—I think it's in one of the visiting teaching lessons—you always ask that question. And my answer should be, "I'm fine," and she would say, "Isn't that nice."

But on that day, something came over me, and I blurted out, "I am going to start buying socks because I will never have time to wash them, and if I do, I'll never have time to match them."

Eileen looked at me, smiled, and said, "Oh, that's nice."

I could have died. I wanted the floor to open and drop me down into the kitchen. I sat through the rest of the meeting just thinking, "Why did you say that? You're the wife of the stake president, and you're hanging out the dirty laundry."

When I went home, I told the boys about it, and they all thought that was funny. They laughed about it as they were cooking their dinner in the microwave.

My husband came home from all his meetings, and he thought it was pretty funny too.

The next morning the phone rang. I heard my husband pick up, and he said, "Well, Eileen, how are you today?" and I gasped. And then the conversation was fairly one-sided. Pretty soon I heard my husband say, "That would be GREAT! Okay!" and he hung up.

"What was that?" I said, kind of uneasy.

He said, "Well, Eileen called, and she said she didn't know what was going on at our house right now, but she thought we might need some help. So she said, 'If I bring dinner every night for the next two weeks, would that help you, President?'"

That was where the "That would be GREAT!" had come from.

Now, if she'd gotten me, I would have said, "Everything's fine. Don't worry, we're fine, no problems here, we're doing just great. I'm sorry I said that yesterday; I was just kidding."

Well, that night, about six o'clock, the doorbell rang. I went to the door, with my sons right behind me hoping that something would be there that they could eat. I opened the door, and Eileen stood there with a tray. She looked at me, and she smiled, and I said, "Come in," and she came into the kitchen and set her tray down on the table. Her doctor husband was right behind her, and he had a tray too.

Now, they had brought Jell-O, which meant they'd thought about this early in the day. They had a cake. None of this KFC stuff. She was just all put together. And she looked at me, and she smiled, and then she said, "Well, we'll see you tomorrow," and off she went.

My boys did not even wait for plates. They got out the forks and the knives and started taking the lids off all of this food. I looked at them and said, "Wait a minute. Here's the deal: We're only going to eat half of it in case she doesn't come back."

Well, you know what? Eileen did come back. She came back every night for two weeks.

Now, this probably wasn't life-changing for Eileen, but it was for me. I didn't know her well, but for someone to be concerned and to reach out and say, "I can help you," that meant a lot. And for her to understand the needs in my home and most of all to say to me, "I don't know you very well, but I love you, and I'm going to feed you what I feed my family," well—I will never forget those two weeks with Eileen. She's one of my dearest friends now. She's one of the people you can call and say, "What have you got in your freezer? I need some help." But more than that, Eileen knows how to love people. She knows how to say to them, "I can help with this." She was standing in for the Lord Jesus Christ, when He said, "I will go before your face. I will be on your right hand and on your left." That was Eileen. "My spirit shall be in your hearts, and mine angels round about you to bear you up" (D&C 84:88). That's what it's all about. •

It's not enough to pray to be an instrument in the hands of the Lord. What I need to be praying for is that every day of my life, I will live in *tune* so the Lord can use me as an *instrument in His hands.* It makes me have to think of my own life often. Are there things that I need to set aside? Are there things that I need to let go? Are there things that I need to be doing differently so that I can be more in tune?

   I have learned that as we live our lives like that, there will be moments when the Lord will use us because He knows that He can have confidence in us.

—EMILY FREEMAN

A Gesture of Love

By
Elaine Dalton

everal years ago, my husband and I were in
Nauvoo. I love going there. And I love getting up early in the morning and running
those streets in silence—thinking and pondering
about what it must have been like to be in Nauvoo
at that time when the Church was just young. Always
I am touched as I run or walk down Parley Street
and read the inscriptions from pioneer journals
that now appear on plaques placed there along that
street. One that always touches me is the notation
that Bathsheba Smith wrote in her journal: "I swept
the floor and put the broom behind the door." In
other words, she left that beautiful home, knowing
that she would never come back to it again, but she
still left it beautiful. And then she said, "I walked
out the door, into an unknown future." So many of

those men and women did that. These were cultured, classy men and women who gave up everything because they knew the gospel was true.

In the weeks prior to my release as the Young Women general president, I often quoted Bathsheba Smith. It was an emotional time, and her words seemed to give me courage to do a hard thing. As I approached my office door to leave the cherished space where much of my time had been spent during the five years I had served in that calling, those words again went through my mind. As I grasped the door handle and was about to close the door, I saw that there behind it in the corner sat a broom. My office staff had placed it there as an unspoken gesture of their love and support. I could not hold back the tears as I realized that it is indeed our faith in the Lord that transports us from one circumstance to another, whatever that may be. •

Sometimes we wonder if anything we're saying to the people that we love and especially to our kids is making a difference. *Is it getting through at all?* I can promise you that it may not be written in their journals, but it will be written in their hearts. Don't give up. Continue to love and to teach.

—HILARY WEEKS

Forgetting Ourselves and Going to Work

By
Virginia H. Pearce

I've been thinking a bit lately about two different orientations. One is couched in language about me: "my happiness," "I can do this myself," "thank you for my life, my blessings, my family."

And then there is the one built around the language of the kingdom—words like "roll forth and fill the earth," "Zion," "one heart," "one mind," and so on.

An article in the *New York Times* (May 20, 2013) by David Brooks chronicles the rising individualism in the United States during the past half century. He quotes a study that found that "between 1960 and 2008 individualistic words and phrases increasingly overshadowed communal words and phrases. That is to say, over those 48 years, words and phrases like 'personalized,' 'self,' 'standout,' unique,' 'I come first,' and 'I can do it myself' were used more frequently. Communal words and phrases like 'community,' 'collective,' 'tribe,' 'share,' 'united,' 'band together' and 'common good' receded."

Like you, I am surrounded and inundated with the culture at large, so when I see trends like that, it's an opportunity to look in the mirror. Undoubtedly the changes in the broader culture are affecting me in how I think and make sense of life. Do those changes match with the culture of Christ—or are they leading me astray?

Think back to the rhetoric of Kirtland and Nauvoo, particularly the language of individuals in journals and letters. There was so much day-to-day fervor around building the kingdom! Even though heartache and personal tragedy and triumph were chronicled, they seemed to coexist with an orientation toward community—an excitement about building Zion, building a people to welcome the Savior.

If this all seems a bit esoteric to you, cast your mind over recent conversations about missionaries. We are all swept up in the increased momentum. Some of our conversation definitely falls into the individualistic orientation: "This will be so much better for boys not to have that year between high school and college to get lost." "This will give girls a more immediate goal." "Missions do amazing things for a person. He or she comes home matured, disciplined, and prepared to succeed."

There's nothing wrong with those conversations. The paradox is, however, that only when a missionary forgets about herself and learns how to focus on taking the gospel to others and building the kingdom—only then does she begin to truly mature and become the person we know she can become.

President Gordon B. Hinckley experienced that change in orientation in the mission field as he responded to his father's advice: "Forget yourself and go to work."

When we forget ourselves—tone down the individualism that we are picking up from the culture at large—and orient ourselves toward truth, toward building the kingdom, magnificent things happen. And the amazing part is that in the Lord's economy, we cannot help but be personally, individually blessed when we orient ourselves toward Him with all our might, mind. and strength.

So, today—right now, this very minute—let's forget about ourselves and go to work! •

When I think of my mother, I always wonder, *how did you do it?* How did you work full time—two jobs, really—nurture, cook, clean, keep us united, manage our home, drive, nurse my sick father, and get him to doctor's appointments here, there, and everywhere? *How did you do it?* It wasn't until I really started to study about the enabling power of the Atonement that I understood where that strength came from. She knew she had a work to do, and Heavenly Father knew she had a most important work to do to keep our family united, and *He gave her the ability to do it far beyond her means.*

—MARY COOK

Love and Warm Towels

By

Carolyn J. Rasmus

My mother lived to be ninety-four. We'd had a lot of differences over the years. There is just something sometimes about a mother and a daughter that doesn't quite click, especially when both are very strong-willed women. But in her later years, I went home to help take care of her. My father had passed away, and she was living with her sister, who was just two years younger.

We had help that came in, but one day I said, "Why don't I just give you a bath?" And so I did. I was a little awkward at first, and she was a little awkward at first. But we got past that, and I remembered that when I was growing up, one of the things my mother would do for me when I took a bath was to hang the towels on the radiator so that they would be warm, and then when she'd hear me get out of the bathtub, she would slip the towel in to me, and it would be all nice and warm. I loved that.

So as we were finishing Mom's bath, I quickly took three towels and ran and put them in the dryer. I helped her get out of the bathtub and sit down on the toilet, and then I ran and got those three hot towels and wrapped her up in them. I looked at her, and she had tears running down her face. She said: "*I* should be taking care of *you*. How did you remember about the towels?"

Well, it was one of those moments when I think all of the hurt and all of the pain went away. I think it was one of those "tender mercies" when the Lord intervened and our hearts were brought together. •

Each one of us has a part to play, and no matter how small or how *insignificant* you think your part is, it matters to the whole. We have something very important to do. *We were born to lead and change the world.*

—ELAINE DALTON

Activating the
Atonement

By
Mariama Kallon

I used to wonder how my life would turn out and even wondered why the Lord saved me. I was raised in Sierra Leone, a country plagued by civil war, and I experienced great sorrows and tragedy. I lost my family, everything I owned, and narrowly escaped death. Yet, as the years have gone by and I've witnessed great miracles, I have come to realize that God watches over all His children. He knows us personally and cares for us one by one. Difficult experiences in life prepare us to recognize God's blessings and to reflect the light of His goodness and love into the lives of others.

None of us is exempt from the sorrows of mortality. Some of us experience the darkness of depression, lose a loved one, or suffer because of the poor choices of others. Too many allow the clouds of fear, bitterness, hatred, and sin to come between them and the peace and happiness God is able to give. Because of the Atonement of Jesus Christ we can overcome these feelings of darkness.

The Savior is able to heal any wound, but we must do our part to access this healing power. I felt tremendous sorrow until I decided to let Him in. To feel the Atonement as an active force in my life, I needed to pray and fast fervently for His guidance. I had to struggle on my knees and ask for courage. I had to live worthy for the Holy Ghost to dwell in me. I also had to ask in faith for a pure heart and a broken and contrite spirit (see Psalm 51:10). Because I was willing to let Him in and turn my life over to Him, He has visited me in mercy.

I had just lost all my family when I became a member of The Church of Jesus Christ of Latter-day Saints and was then able to serve a full-time mission in the Salt Lake City Temple Square Mission. As I have reached out to others, I have learned more about myself and recognized ways I can be better. The patience, forgiveness, and humility gained through our trials help us to become more like God. And if we allow Him, God will consecrate the bitter times in our lives for more good than we can imagine.

I know with all my heart that He is a loving God, a God who keeps His promises. I have seen great miracles and therefore my soul will rejoice in my God, the rock of my salvation. I will not allow my burdens to destroy my peace (see 2 Nephi 4:26–30).

God lives, and He loves all of His children. The Atonement of Jesus Christ is real. Do not be discouraged by the turmoil and pains of this world and life.

Let us live each day by striving to do the best we can with a positive attitude. Have faith in Him and be of good cheer. He is with us and will stand by us. •

I Am a Duck

By
Sandra Turley

I was driving down a country road with my four children in the car. It was a beautiful, calm day. As we drove, I started to feel nauseated. A few minutes later, I had no choice but to pull over on the side of the road and crank up the air conditioner, as the car seemed so unbearably hot. I crawled into the backseat of the car to lie down on the floor between the children. My entire body began to go numb. My six-year-old announced over and over that he needed to use the bathroom. My five-year-old passed out Tic-Tacs. My baby was crying. My eight-year-old found my cell phone and began to call for help.

I didn't know what was happening to my body; it felt like it was going away. It was hard to breathe. It was hard to think clearly. I had only scary thoughts: maybe my body was going to go completely away.

Maybe I was dying. My hands froze in a strange position and I had no control or ability to move them. I listened to my eight-year-old call a dear friend to come help. I then listened as she tearfully spoke to the 911 operators and told them that her mommy was hurting. Our friend arrived to take the kids, and an ambulance came to take me. Though I didn't know what was happening to my body, the ER doctor fairly quickly declared my symptoms as an anxiety attack and told me to go home and rest.

This is new territory for me. I am generally a happy person who loves to make other people happy. I had never thought of the word *anxiety* as it relates to me. At times I have claimed words like *overwhelmed, worried, easily agitated, emotional,* and *depressed.* But I had never claimed the word *anxiety* as part of me. Looking back, I certainly had major depression during our struggle with infertility. That depression went unnamed and untreated. I suffered alone. I have dealt with mild depression symptoms through my childbearing years. Between children three and four, I finally addressed my symptoms with prescribed medication, homeopathic supplements, extreme dietary changes, and plenty of prayerful soul searching.

I even took up drinking—diet Dr Pepper—to help keep me going. Everything seemed to be in balance.

Apparently it wasn't.

It felt like I had all these balls up in the air and none of them were falling, so everything was okay. But then everything fell at once. If my body had told me to slow down in any less dramatic way, I would not have listened. I am so grateful for my anxiety attack. Because of it, I *stopped, studied,* and *surrendered,* and I have been *saved.*

Stopped: I have a kamikaze personality. If something is scary, I just jump in headfirst before really thinking so that I can just get it done. Sadly, this usually works out for me. So I say "Yes" to everything that comes my way and will flounder silently rather than admit defeat. This is not wise. After I came home from the ER, I tearfully canceled all of my extra responsibilities for the following two months (performances, church responsibilities, school responsibilities, everything). I also stopped holding my smartphone. I stopped looking at it and stopped being a slave to it. Freedom. I left only six responsibilities on my list, and their names were Ava, Davis, Ella, Gwen, Josh, and me.

Studied: I studied about anxiety. I accepted the

title and ultimately learned that my struggles with "depression" in the past were not actually depression, but anxiety. It feels good to have the right diagnosis so that I can work correctly to heal.

Surrendered: After studying and learning as much as I could, I still didn't feel right. I finally realized I couldn't fix this on my own. In addition to praying and seeking greater spiritual strength, I went to a therapist. I wish I had taken the time to work with a therapist *years* ago. I trusted her immediately. I surrendered to her expertise, and I vulnerably worked to understand the root cause of my anxiety. She gave me tools that I use every day. Tools to stop my thoughts and assess them. Tools to address my people-pleasing and overachieving nature. Tools to train my mind to stay in the present. Tools to rearrange our habits as a family at home. Tools to notice my triggers, to slow them down and stop them before the debilitating anxiety takes over. *This is a work in progress*. I have a long way to go. But it is worth it for my health and for the happiness of our family.

Saved: My Savior is the only one who understands the exact cause of my hurt and struggles of my soul. He alone has already suffered for both my sin and my pain. After all that I could do to heal myself, I turned to Him in faith to heal the rest of my ache. He helped me *stop, study,* and *surrender,* and He alone *saves* me. And you.

There are so many components to my situation, just as there are for yours. But even speaking about the generalities of our hurt gives us a place to understand that we are not "weird" if we are suffering from mental illness. Each day, new environmental and social factors contribute to a massive increase in mental hurt in our society. There is so much hurt, it can no longer be a purely private battle that we hide beneath the surface.

Ducks make life look so effortless on the surface. Their apparent serenity makes those of us who are struggling to stay afloat feel even more incapable. To some extent, everyone is a duck. We all have something difficult hiding underneath. So from one duck to another, though I do not know what is going on underneath your surface, I pray for your healing, and I know that through Christ's *saving* Atonement we can all find the peace we seek in the present. •

When things are not going right for you, when you feel distant from Jesus Christ, hold on. I can remember days when I've been teaching and I felt so unprepared and so inadequate that I couldn't even get myself to open up the scriptures and read them—so I would *hold on* to them. I think that's what Jesus Christ is saying to every one of us: "Come unto me. Let me heal you." I have the sense that we're going to get someday to the other side, and we're going to have new understanding given to us, and we're going to say, "You mean, I didn't have to do it all by myself? *You were there?*"

—CAROLYN J. RASMUS

His Power to Redeem

By
Wendy Ulrich

Think of something in your past, something that part of you wishes you could undo. Perhaps it was a failure or a sin; perhaps it was a loss, or just something really painful. And now ask yourself this question: What is something you learned from that experience that you will never forget and that makes you a better person today?

Here are some responses I have heard from women: I learned compassion. I learned not to judge. I learned patience. I learned that God truly loves me. I learned strength. I learned perseverance. I learned humility. I learned faith.

Isn't it interesting that these are the very things we came to mortality to learn, that help us become more like God? I assert that it is the Atonement of Christ that makes that learning and growth possible for every single one of His children, whether they know anything about Christ or not. But for those of us who are His disciples, we especially can afford to give up all hope of ever having a better past because we understand Christ's amazing, vast power to redeem.

In fact, I believe His power to redeem is SO great that regardless of what has happened or whose fault it is or how deeply it hurts, He can make us better for it—not just good enough, not just enough to squeak by, but the best person we are capable personally of being is still within our reach if we turn to Him and trust Him when He says, "I have the power to forgive and to redeem everything I allow to happen to you." •

There will be reasons for us to be
discouraged and despondent and in
despair. That's all part of mortality. But
when we realize the battle and where we
find our strength, we can keep going,
and we will have all that we need.

—ARDETH KAPP

Watching Over
Your Heart

By
Kris Belcher

I'm normally the one who jokes around and finds the humor during difficult situations. But recently I experienced a challenge in which I did very little laughing and a whole lot of weeping. I was hospitalized twice in one month with a systemic staph infection. The staph lodged itself in my backside, which prevented me from moving much. Man, talk about pain in the bum!

I was in constant and severe pain for weeks, and no medication sufficiently alleviated my agony. I hurt so bad for so long that I began to wonder if I would ever heal. There were so many medical tests, so many doctors, and so much pain that I didn't think I could handle one more second of it all. My prayers were a continual, "Please, please help me!"

One night, when I was in tremendous pain, I lay

on my hospital bed and wept. I was sweating like I was running a marathon, and it was hard to breathe. When I pushed the nurse's call button, no one came in my room to assist me, and I pled with Father in Heaven for help.

In walked James, my husband, who immediately got someone in to administer some pain medication. My prayer had been answered.

But the trouble wasn't over. When the nurse's aide came in to take my vitals, I knew something was wrong. All of a sudden, the whole cardiac team was in my room. I had a gazillion leads placed on my chest and monitors displaying my heart activity. The crash cart was even there by my bed. I felt like I was in some TV medical drama. If I weren't blind, I would have looked around for George Clooney.

When the doctor came in, he informed me that while my heart rate was usually in the 90s, it was now at 240 and showed no signs of slowing. He was going to administer some medication that would slow down and possibly stop my heart so that they could restart it to pump at a normal level.

Two nurses each held a syringe, ready to put into my IV. I truly wondered if I was going to die. If they stopped my heart, would it start again?

Before giving the order to administer the medication, the doctor asked me to try a certain muscle contraction, which can sometimes slow down the heart. I was able to follow his instructions, and my heart immediately slowed to a normal rate. There was an audible sigh of relief in my room from the whole medical team, but no one was as relieved as I was.

I was kept on monitors, and, at one point that evening, a nurse came in and introduced herself to me, saying, "I'll be the one watching over your heart tonight."

I almost cried at her words. She was the one monitoring my heart activity, but the Spirit let me know who was really watching over my heart that night. And every night. Heavenly Father was completely aware of my condition and watching over me.

Our circumstances are different. Our pains, trials, worries, sorrows, and other personal struggles may not be the same. But there is one thing each of us can be assured of. You and I have a Father who loves and knows us personally. He knows how much we hurt. He knows our longings and hears our desperate prayers. He may not always deliver us from the pain and heartbreak, but He always helps us through it.

When it feels like your heart is breaking, I invite you to turn to Him again and again to feel the peace and love you need. There is no other source for lasting healing. •

There is no religion, no
science, no philosophy, no
history, no art that offers
people the privilege of
absolute certainty in all
things. True religion is not
only about offering answers
to our questions but also
about giving us *courage
to face the unknown with
calm humility and faith.*

—WENDY ULRICH

Answers to My Cries

By
Macy Robison

When my daughter was a newborn, my husband and I would drop what we were doing and go right away when she would cry. She was so little and inexperienced. We knew she was crying because she really needed something, and because we knew we could help, we came to her rescue.

But as she got a bit older, we learned that helping her right away when she cried wasn't always the best thing for her. Some experiences with nighttime feedings made that abundantly clear. So, we let her cry sometimes. Because sometimes (especially in the middle of the night) what she wanted wasn't what she needed. And in those times, even though we still heard her, we were helping her the most when we didn't run to her rescue right away. We were helping her the most when we let her figure things out for herself.

It's interesting to me that in the scriptures, prayer is often referred to as a cry. In Alma 34, for instance, we're specifically instructed to cry unto the Lord. We are to cry in our fields, over all our flocks, in our houses, and over our household at morning, midday, and evening. (That seems like a lot of crying to me, but perhaps that's just my perspective as the mother of a toddler talking.)

When I was small, I remember that my cries to the Lord were almost always answered. As I've grown and gained experience, sometimes my prayers feel like unanswered cries in the night that no one can hear. But I've learned that isn't true. My cries are always heard. My Heavenly Father always hears me. And because our Father in Heaven is perfect, I know that my cries don't tire him out like my daughter's earthly cries tire me. As His daughter, I need to remember that just because I'm not getting the answer I want, it doesn't mean I'm not heard. It just means that maybe the thing that I'm crying and praying for isn't coming to pass because it isn't the best for me. Or maybe I need to wait a little longer. Or maybe I just need to figure it out for myself. •

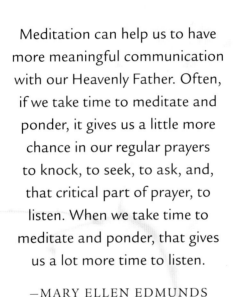

Meditation can help us to have more meaningful communication with our Heavenly Father. Often, if we take time to meditate and ponder, it gives us a little more chance in our regular prayers to knock, to seek, to ask, and, that critical part of prayer, to listen. When we take time to meditate and ponder, that gives us a lot more time to listen.

—MARY ELLEN EDMUNDS

Recently I conducted an experiment. For thirty days during my morning prayers, I asked Heavenly Father what was most important for me to accomplish that day. After my prayer, I would listen and wait to allow the Spirit to speak to me about what was most important to do that day. Usually it was a prompting of only one thing. He didn't send a long list of things to do—just one, maybe two.

One morning I felt prompted to write my nine-year old-daughter, Meg, a note telling her how much I loved her. After dinner, I finally got around to writing the note. I left it on her bed while she was taking a bath. After getting out of the bath and getting into her pajamas, she came downstairs where I was. She was crying, really crying. I asked her what was wrong. Meg told me that she had been feeling very lonely and had just been upstairs praying for Heavenly Father to help her to feel loved. She went into her room and found my note. She could barely get the words out while she was telling the story. I was grateful to know what was most important that day.

—HILARY WEEKS

Defining Faith

By
Jenny Oaks Baker

Wh
en my wonderful mother-in-law was diagnosed with cancer, our family's fervent prayers for her recovery made me think back on the experience of praying for my own dear mother's recovery from the same illness fourteen years earlier. When I was twenty-two, my mother was diagnosed with cancer. I learned the devastating news while on a Study Abroad at the BYU Jerusalem Center. When I received that call, I was standing at a pay phone on the banks of the Sea of Galilee. I was in the land where the Lord had performed so many miracles, and I knew He could heal my mother. I just needed to have enough faith!

I prayed and prayed in faith for her recovery, but I started to wonder about the relationship between faith and the Lord's will. Before I returned home from Israel, I felt impressed to email my father, Elder Dallin Oaks, the following question:

"How can we have faith that someone will get well, or something will happen, when we know that everything is dependent upon the Lord's will?"

He responded as follows: "I believe that the only true faith is faith in the Lord Jesus Christ. Everything we have 'faith' in is based on faith or trust in the Lord Jesus Christ (and His Father), that they will do what is best for us (another way of saying according to their will in our behalf). Therefore, we cannot really say that we have 'faith' that the Lord will do what we ask Him to do in any and all circumstances. There will be times when that is not even right for us. If we place our trust in Him, that is what we should do. And He has taught us that we should pray for those we love, and should pray for those who are sick. We do that, and exercise our faith in the Lord, and that is what we are supposed to do.

"I have seen people punish themselves greatly because they prayed in faith for the recovery of a person who dies, and then considered that they had 'let them die' because their own faith was insufficient to bring about the desired result. My mother felt that feeling of guilt for many years after the death of my father, until she came to see that she was not at fault in his death. It was the will of the Lord, and she had done all she could."

My father's explanation enabled me to put my faith and trust in the Lord as I dealt with my mother's illness and eventual death nearly one year later. I had prayed for her recovery, but I knew that it was the Lord's will that she return to Him, and I trusted in Him. Through the entire process my faith and testimony were strengthened.

Since my mother-in-law was also called home, I have been so grateful that my husband and I were able to teach our own children to have faith in the Lord and to trust in His will as we struggled through this difficult time. I know that the Lord loves us, and I am so very grateful for the plan of salvation! I know we will all be reunited again. I thank Heavenly Father for making it possible for families to be together forever, and for giving us the knowledge of this eternal truth. •

Members of most Christian faiths, including mine, believe in personal revelation. We believe that we can ask God for help SPECIFICALLY for our own family. We believe that He will send answers.

Do you believe this is true for you? And if it is, is it also true for your neighbor? And if God is speaking to you AND your neighbor, do you believe, possibly, that He could be guiding you in DIFFERENT ways as parents?

No matter what parenting method or issue is popular for families at the moment, God is waiting to reveal truth to you about YOUR family. Because God chose YOU to be the parent of a specific child, He will make sure you have the answers needed for that child. And not only will God's plan differ from family to family, but it may very well differ from one of your own children to the next. This is why parenting MUST be driven and guided by the Spirit and not the world.

—WHITNEY PERMANN

Answers I Didn't Recognize

By
Emily Watts

ometimes I assume Heavenly Father is not answering my prayers, when maybe He really is, and I just didn't recognize the answer. Has that ever happened to you? You think, "Why doesn't He listen? Why won't He pay attention to me?" when suddenly you realize that He was answering all along and you just didn't see.

Our two oldest children got their mission calls at the same time, the same day. A week or two before they were supposed to go, my daughter was working desperately to get our house and yard looking better than they ever did in our real lives so that we could have people over to say good-bye. We had a ton of family coming, and so she was working hard. She drove our van to an uncle's house to pick up an edger for the lawn, and on the way home she misinterpreted a traffic light and turned left in front of an oncoming vehicle and was broadsided. The van flipped on its side, skidded into the median, slid into a bus, and finally came to a stop. And I got a phone call.

I thought, "Heavenly Father, this little girl who has been trying so hard to decide whether to go on a mission in the first place, who finally made the decision, who is going to the temple THIS WEEKEND—why didn't You protect her? You couldn't have put in her mind, 'Don't turn left in front of oncoming traffic'? You couldn't have helped her see that light? Don't You care?"

Let me tell you the rest of the story.

After the van came to a stop, my daughter climbed out of it and ran to see what had happened to the occupants of the other car. They had airbags, so they were okay, and they said, "Please don't worry about us; go see what happened to the driver of the van."

She said, "I was the driver of the van."

They were aghast. "How is that possible? How are you walking?" They made her sit down on the curb. She had a pretty good scrape on her arm because the window had been open and her arm had been out the window as the van skidded across the road, but there didn't seem to be anything else wrong with her.

Interestingly, the windshield of that van had recently been replaced, and because the company doing the repair didn't have the right kit to glue it in they had just installed it in a sort of rubber gasket all around the edges. As soon as the van was hit, the windshield popped right out and landed on the ground. Not one shard of glass came in.

Interestingly, the captain's chairs in the middle section of that van had recently been rotated around because my kids had been playing a game, and the captain's chair was completely blocking the side window, so no glass came in that side of the van.

Interestingly, our van was essentially folded in half, totaled, such that when the emergency crews came on the scene they assumed they would need to call LifeFlight. Instead they found my daughter sitting on the curb with a scrape on her arm.

I can almost hear Heavenly Father say, "What makes you think I wasn't protecting her? What makes you think I wasn't answering that prayer? Here's a fact of life, Daughter—if you turn left in front of a car, chances are, you're going to get hit. But because I have a special mission in mind for your little girl, I'm going to protect her from the worst of the consequences and let this be a lesson instead."

It doesn't always work that way, but I'm guessing that kind of thing happens more often than we know. He guides and protects my children more than I will ever know or understand. He guides and protects me, too. Our prayers are answered. ●

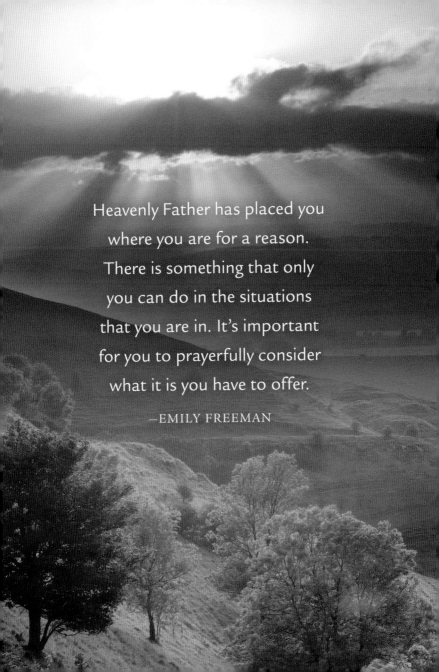

Heavenly Father has placed you
where you are for a reason.
There is something that only
you can do in the situations
that you are in. It's important
for you to prayerfully consider
what it is you have to offer.

—EMILY FREEMAN

I know what it's like to pray that the Lord will be there to lift you up. You know what it's like. You've been there on your knees many a time when you've looked up and said to your Father in Heaven, "Are you really there? I need some help right now."

For the most part, He doesn't reach down and reconfigure everything. For the most part, He works by eternal rules because He doesn't worry so much about the mortality of what's going on as He does how we're feeling about it and how we're dealing with it and what we can learn from it.

And so there is a sense of peace that comes into our hearts. There's a sense of serenity in spite of the turmoil around us that helps us to look up into the face of God with hope and with faith.

—HEIDI SWINTON

Learning to Depend on Him

By
Hilary Weeks

I used to be pretty terrified of performing in front of people; I always have been. I loved writing music, and I loved being in my living room playing it, and I loved recording it in the studio. It's just that getting up in front of people and performing it, which is part of the deal, really terrified me. I used to worry months before a performance. I would get that pit in my stomach, and every time I would think about the upcoming performance I would panic, and that fear would go through my whole body. I would worry about everything: What if I sang the wrong notes? What if I messed up the words? What if I needed to cough in the middle of a line? What if I spontaneously combusted during the middle of a song?

Every time, that fear led me to my knees, where I

pleaded with Heavenly Father to help me and to get me through it and to make my voice strong so that I could sing. And every time, that prayer was answered. It didn't mean that I didn't make mistakes—I did—but He got me through it every time.

But I would wonder, Why would He give me a talent or a gift and then allow me to be so afraid of using it? I realized through the years it was so that I would learn to depend on Him, so that I would turn to Him because there WAS no other source to get through it, and that I would learn that He was there for me. He taught me personally that our weaknesses can become our strengths.

I testify to you that when we are on our knees, or when we are walking down the street or driving in our car, He hears us, and He knows us and He loves us and He'll answer our prayers. •

In a world of quick pleasures, we should turn to the Lord first and often to fill our souls with the goodness and nourishment He freely offers.

—SANDRA TURLEY

Love and Pancakes

By

Mary Cook

I became part of the Cook family as a stepmother over twenty-six years ago. My husband had been widowed and had a well-established family of four adult children and eight grandchildren under the age of eight. I remember well a particularly hard day in the early part of our marriage when my husband, Richard, said, "Mary, you have to understand that right now you're out of the Cook tent, and you may never be fully in." Well, I took that comment as a great challenge!

It was an overwhelming experience for all of us at first. Like most families, the Cooks had their traditions, their recipes, and their ways of doing things. So I went to where my heart felt most comfortable— the grandchildren. I had been an elementary school teacher, and children had always been easy for me to love. That first year of marriage had its challenges, but gradually, as I sought out the hearts of the grandchildren, the tent door started to crack open.

Since three of the four children lived out of state, we had large family gatherings at our home in Park City. The little ones were always the first to awaken, so I made an effort to make breakfast an "event." As a child, my mother would make pancakes in the shape of a cat. I started with cats, then expanded my repertoire with requests such as: "Can you make me a giraffe?" "How about a Tyrannosaurus Rex?" I am not an artist, but I was pretty good at convincing little ones I could make anything! We would laugh and use our imaginations to determine what my mistakes were. (They still say Michael Jordan dunking the basketball was my greatest feat.) Breakfast and animal pancakes became a bonding experience for us.

Recently, I got a text from three of those little ones, now grown and attending BYU. "Hey, we're in Park City and it looks like it might snow. May we come over and stay?" As young coeds do, they arrived late that night, after we had gone to bed.

The next morning I heard stirrings in the kitchen,

so I went in to greet them and asked, "What would you like for breakfast?"

Timidly Lauren asked, "Would you make us animal pancakes?"

I had been working on a presentation, so, in the midst of making an elephant and an iguana, I asked them their thoughts about how we acquire and keep a testimony. They gave me some very interesting insights on that question, especially as it relates in the lives of young adults.

Several years ago, I knew my efforts were appreciated when from out of nowhere Richard said, "Mary, my children love you. I think you've made it into the tent!"

S ome galaxies contain 100 trillion stars. (That's more than the national debt!) But it is estimated that there may be more than 170 billion galaxies, each of those with all those trillions of stars. In October 2013, a galaxy was discovered that is approximately 13.1 billion light-years from the earth. (A light-year is almost 6 trillion miles.) All this does blow my mind. But just because I don't understand it doesn't mean it isn't true.

Listen to the One who created the stars and the galaxies and all: "The heavens, they are many, and they cannot be numbered unto man; but they are numbered unto me, for they are mine" (Moses 1:37). If He knows each star, He knows each you. Stars are miracles. You are a miracle. You are absolutely unique. You are loved individually for who you are, not for who anybody else is. You are known so well and cherished so much.

—MARY ELLEN EDMUNDS

For Love's Sake

By
Emily Freeman

S ome years ago, my husband and I were called into our bishop's office. He told us of a family who were facing serious difficulties, and one of their sons was really struggling. The boy was about to be kicked out of junior high; it was the third school he had been expelled from. The bishop asked, "Is there something we could do to help in this situation?" Among other issues, Garett struggled with a severe learning disability that made it hard for him to do his homework unsupervised. On top of that, he filled up his idle moments by vandalizing our neighborhood. As we brainstormed, we came up with a solution. We decided to ask three families if they would be willing to do homework help with him and feed him dinner.

For the next four years we invited Garett into our

homes at night for dinner, and then helped him with his homework. On the day he graduated from high school there were three moms who wanted to walk through the line with him when he got his diploma; I was one of the three.

The summer after Garett graduated was a really hard one. He made some bad choices and even ended up in prison for a short time. Toward the end of the summer, my husband was driving down the street, and he saw Garett standing on the curb in front of his home with all of his belongings. He pulled down the street a couple of blocks and called me, saying, "Garett is standing on the curb with all of his belongings. What do you want me to do?"

I thought about it for a moment. I had two daughters who lived at home: a senior and a ninth grader. I knew that Garett had been using drugs, that he had been in prison, and that there were other addictions he was fighting. I was worried about bringing that into my home. But I knew the Lord would know what to do. So I prayed. The answer came clearly: *Bring him home.*

Before Garett unpacked I sat him down on the couch and explained what the rules would be if he chose to live in our home: go to church, pay your tithing, get a job. There were other conditions also: no talking to his former friends ever again, no Facebook, and he would have to turn in his phone every night at 10:00 p.m. I told him there wouldn't be any warnings. If he didn't want to accept those conditions, we would help him find somewhere else to live.

What I thought wouldn't last for longer than three weeks turned into three years. It wasn't easy, but it has been a journey that has blessed all of our lives. I won't forget one particularly hard evening. At the time we were struggling to know how to help Garett. That night I was visiting an art museum. While we were there, I came upon a beautiful painting of the Savior. I stood right in front of that picture and reflected upon our situation for a long, long time. As I looked into the eyes of the Savior, I remember asking, "What is it that I need to do now? What is my job?" The task at hand seemed so great that it felt as if it would overwhelm me.

The answer came back clearly: "To love him. That's it: To love him. That's all I need you to do. I will do the rest."

In that moment I was reminded of the great commandments—to love God and to love our neighbor.

To love. When I look back at this journey, perhaps that is the most profound lesson the Lord has taught me. Through Garett, the Lord taught me how to love.

Now Garett is active in the Church, he has a job, and he is attending college and playing football. More important, he has had a great influence on many people—a profound influence. His story is a reminder that when we turn our hearts to the Lord, He can change our lives. There have been many who have found the courage to change because they have seen the change in Garett.

In fact, a few years after Garett moved in, I opened my front door to find a young man standing there with tears running down his cheeks. He asked if the "coach" was around. My husband, Greg, is the coach of a high school lacrosse team, and boys come over on a regular basis to talk with him. After Ian left, Greg came to tell me, "Ian said he wants to turn his life around. He wants to start going to church. He saw what Garett did in his life, and he wants to do that. He wants to know if we'd be willing to help him."

So Ian joined our family. It was a remarkable experience having him with us. He came to church with us and ultimately received a mission call to the Indiana Indianapolis Mission.

Just before Ian left for his mission, we had a conversation that left a deep impression on my heart. He said, "You know, me and Garett always thought you were for us, but have you ever wondered if maybe we were for you?"

I turned to him and replied, "Ian, you don't know how profound that statement is."

My life has been changed because of those two boys. I have learned lessons I wouldn't have learned in any other way if I had not opened my heart and my home to them. Most important, I learned what it is to love as the Savior loves—to love for love's sake. •

Sometimes the way we look on the outside gives no indication whatsoever of what we are feeling on the inside. And perhaps there is even nobody who really knows the unseen wounds that you carry in your heart. My prayer would be that if you deal with any kind of pain—whether it is physical, spiritual, emotional, whatever the cause—if you carry disappointments, if you feel lonely, that somehow you would feel the love of Jesus Christ for you.

—CAROLYN J. RASMUS

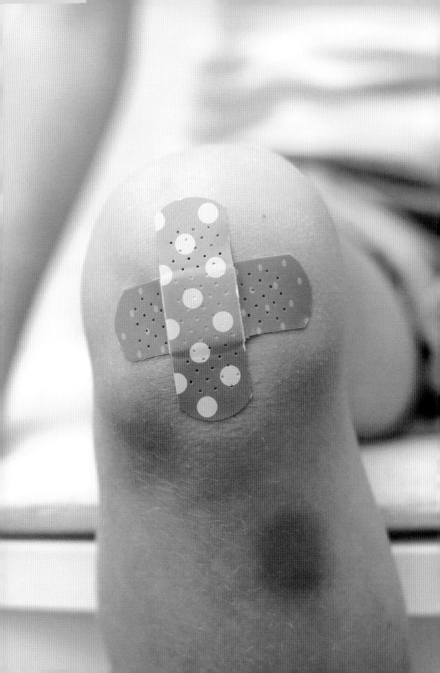

Love and Agency

By
Chieko Okazaki

I have a grandson named Kenzo, and when he was about two and a half years old, his parents, Ken and Kelly, were discussing something in the living room, and Kenzo kept interrupting them with such statements of his own. Kelly finally stopped and said: "Kenzo, you mustn't interrupt people when they are talking. It's impolite, so that's a rule we should make in our family. You need to sit quietly while Dad and I are talking. Do you understand this rule?"

Kenzo said, "Yes," and sat quietly while they continued talking. But after a while, he said, "Mom, I'm upset."

Kelly and Ken looked at him in surprise. He'd been so quiet that they'd almost forgotten that he was there. And Kelly asked quietly and gently, "What are you upset about, Kenzo?"

Kenzo answered, "I'm upset about that rule. When you are talking, I want to talk too."

Now, my son Ken is an attorney, so he spends a lot of time thinking about issues of fairness and justice. Both he and Kelly immediately saw that Kenzo was asserting his right to be treated as a person, that in a slightly different setting, with slightly older people, this could be an issue of interpreting the free speech clause of the first amendment that could be a U.S. Supreme Court case. So they apologized to Kenzo and told him that they needed to change the rule. They explained that the rule should not be that the adults got to talk and children didn't get to talk. Instead, the rule needed to be: first, that everybody needed to talk about the same topic; and second, that you couldn't start talking when someone else was already talking, but you needed to wait for a pause so that everybody else could listen to what you were saying.

Kenzo understood these rules perfectly. I don't know whether the content of the conversation has improved markedly around the household, but I know that the communication certainly has.

Now, I think it's pretty remarkable that Kenzo, at two and a half, could tell how and what he was feeling. And he had words to explain those feelings instead of just having one of those famous two-year-old tantrums. But I also think it's pretty remarkable that the two adults in the room realized that they had something to learn from this two-year-old to make their family become better. This was a situation in which honoring the agency of everyone involved also increased the amount of love in the family. •

At a recent family reunion, we had a chance to hear memories of my great-grandfather voiced by his last remaining grandchildren, of whom there were ten (from an original fifty), ranging in age from a remarkably spry 79 to an unbelievably spry 99. A chapel full of descendants, representing only a small percentage of those eligible to be there, awoke in my heart an unbounded gratitude for the opportunity to belong to these good people in some way. And that uncovered a bright chain of blessings going

clear back to the basic plan of salvation our Father laid out for us—that we were not merely His creations but His family, linked to each other in ways that transcend anything mortality can throw at us. The most powerful Being in the universe holds in His heart for each one of us the concern of a tender parent. Whether life is weighing me down or letting me fly on any particular day seems immaterial in the face of such a truth.

—EMILY WATTS

Encircled in Their Loving Arms

By
Barbara Thompson

I t wasn't until I was in college that I had an experience that really rooted and grounded me in the love of our Heavenly Father and our Savior. A long, long time ago, when I was attending Brigham Young University in Provo, Utah, the Provo Temple was being built. The Provo Temple was only the fifteenth temple in the Church, and so you can see we've come a long way.

When the temple was finished and it was about to be dedicated, this was a great event. I had never had the opportunity in my lifetime to attend a temple dedication, and I was really excited—as were thousands of other students who were attending BYU.

We all wanted the opportunity to attend the dedication, and we were told that if we would see our bishop and get a special ticket, we could attend this dedication. Obviously, there wasn't enough room in the Provo Temple for all of these thousands of people who wanted to attend. So for this special day, they made the Marriott Center an "annex" to the temple, actually a part of the temple for that particular day. The Marriott Center is a huge arena that holds more than 20,000 people, and I had attended basketball games there, had gone to concerts and other programs, devotionals, forums. I had been to many things there, but never had I seen it as part of the temple.

We were asked to prepare ourselves, to come to the temple dedication fasting, and I tried to prepare myself in every way for this special occasion.

On the day we got there, we were there quite early, and for an hour, they asked us to just sit quietly, not talk or visit with anyone. In those days we didn't have the distractions of cell phones or other electronic devices, and so I was just sitting there quietly. And during that time, I honestly felt as if my Heavenly Father and my Savior were sitting on either side of me, expressing their love to me. I will never, ever forget how that felt. I truly felt encircled in their loving arms. It was a testimony to me of the reality of their love for me.

It was so vivid in my memory that even forty years later I can still remember how that felt. I'd never had such a wonderful feeling in all my life. As I think back on that time, I realize that with that assurance that Heavenly Father loved me, I was able to get through many tough experiences. There were times when I was discouraged or felt alone or thought I couldn't do what needed to be done, and I would recall that experience. When I had hard times in college, or in my career, or even in dating (I did have a couple of dates)—all the times when you just felt like you needed something more to be able to sustain you—I could remember that time. And when there were tough decisions to be made, or when there were family concerns, or when there was a death of a loved one, all these times I was able to look back on that experience and know that Heavenly Father loves me. ●

No matter our situation in life, our loving Father is watching over us. He knows our challenges and heartbreaks and is right there to remind us of our premortal tutoring. No one is excluded from His sight, His knowledge, and, most importantly, from His love.

—KRIS BELCHER

Photo Credits

vi: daizuoxin/shutterstock.com

2: Rafal Olkis/shutterstock.com

7: macknimal/shutterstock.com

9: bobloblaw/istockphoto/
Thinkstock

10: 2Frogs Studio/shutterstock.com

13: Andrekart Photography/
shutterstock.com

14: Alexander Kuguchin/
shutterstock.com

16: Baranova Anna/
shutterstock.com

20: Ryhor Bruyeu/istock

22: moodboard/Thinkstock

27: Mikael Damkier/
shutterstock.com

28: Xiebiyun/shutterstock.com

30: 8ran/istock

34: iravgustin/shutterstock.com

36: hxdyl/shutterstock.com

40: Pavelk/shutterstock.com

42: cmcderm1/istock

46: taden/istock

48: Andrekart Photography/
shutterstock.com

51: happydancing/shutterstock.com

52: Flas100/shutterstock.com

54: L.Trott/shutterstock.com

60: omersukrugoksu/istock

62: Alexey V Smirnov/
shutterstock.com

65: anawat sudchanham/
shutterstock.com

66: Ragne Kabanova/
shutterstock.com

70: Andrekart Photography/
shutterstock.com

72: mama_mia/shutterstock.com

75: OlegDoroshin/shutterstock.com

76: OlafSpeier/istock

78: Alta Oosthuizen/
shutterstock.com

82: edwardolive/istock

88: Rike_/istock

90: FlamingPumpkin/istock